Library of
Davidson College

A Circus of Needs

Books by Stephen Dunn

Looking for Holes in the Ceiling (1974)
Full of Lust and Good Usage (1976)
A Circus of Needs (1978)

A Circus of Needs

poems by

Stephen Dunn

Carnegie-Mellon University Press
Pittsburgh & London 1978

Acknowledgements

Acknowledgement is made to editors of the following magazines in which some of these poems have appeared: *The American Poetry Review, the Antioch Review, The Aspen Magazine, The Back Door, The Chowder Review, Dacotah Territory, December, The Denver Quarterly, Epoch, The Greenfield Review, Iowa Review, The Massachusetts Review, The Nation, New Letters, The North American Review, The North Stone Review, Poetry Now, Poetry Northwest, Poetry on the Buses (Pittsburgh), Prairie Schooner, Three Rivers Poetry Journal,* and *Quarterly West.*

"Essay on Sanity" won first prize in the 1976 Hellric House Poetry Contest.

"The Magician's Dream", "The Gambler at Home", and "The Man Who Never Loses His Balance" won *Poetry Northwest's* Theodore Roethke Prize in 1977.

I am indebted to Ira Sadoff for the title "A Concise History of the Future".

Library of Congress Catalog Card Number: 78-59800
ISBN 0-915604-50-7
ISBN 0-915604-15-9 Pbk.
Copyright © 1978 by Stephen Dunn
All rights reserved
Printed and bound in the United States of America
First Edition

And perhaps man's real name, the emblem of his being, is Desire. For what is Heidegger's temporality or Machado's 'otherness', what is man's continuous casting himself toward which is not he himself, if not Desire?

—Octavio Paz

for Howard & Jody Mohr;
Al & Arlie Zolynas

Contents

Homage to the Divers   9

I

Midnight   13
The Man Who Never Loses His Balance   15
The Capitalist's Love Letter   16
Split: 1962   17
Outline For a Religious Story   18
For A., Who Knows It's Somewhere
  in the Vicinity of the Heart   19
Scenario   20
If Once In Silence   22
Any Time   23
Building a Person   24
Beached Whales Off Margate   26
Belly Dancer at the Hotel Jerome   27
The Muse   28
The Gambler at Home   29
Directions   30
Greenwich Village: A Memory   32
Sister   34
Tortures   36
A Concise History of the Future   37
Notes Toward a 20th Century Newsreel   39
Here and There   40
A Circus of Needs   41

II

Weatherman   45
Imagine: A Stolen Kiss   47
Anatomy Lesson: A School For Boys   48
Let's See If I Have it Right   49
Essay on Sanity   50
Argument   54

III

In a Dream of Horses   59
Backyard   60
Modern Fable   61
Introduction to the 20th Century   62
Creating the Conditions   63
The Magician's Dream   65
Danse Manhattanique   66
The Manhattanite's Dream   67
Let's Say   68
This Late In the Century   70
A Few Nights and Days   71
Fable of the Unsharable Secrets of the Universe   74
Fable of the Water Merchants   75
Fable of the Mad and the Respectable   76
The Man Who Loves Hegel   77
Dream   78
Modern Dance Class   79
The Obsession   81
The Worrier   83
The Solitary Man's Story   85
To You, Whomever   87
Contact   89
Instead of You   90

Homage to the Divers

*A love poem at the bottom
of the sea, in a treasure ship,
reachable, yes,
we must believe reachable.
In an air-tight container
somewhere in the captain's quarters,
somewhere off Hatteras,
written by . . .
And a key in a skeleton's hand
and the whole world up above
diving for it,
some with all the equipment,
some holding their breath.*

I

Midnight

Midnight in some midnight place.
And here the welcome dark
after a good day, the slight discomfort
of the six o'clock news.
In certain places midnight accumulates
at the end of a beggar's wrists:
ask for the time
and that's what time it is.
What can I do but laugh
when I light a small lamp
in the basement and my daughter complains
"You put the light on
too dark down there".
She's always asleep at midnight,
she wakes in a bed surrounded
by posters of kittens.
Someday I'll have to tell her privilege
is what gets taken away.
People deep in midnight,
that's all they think about—
taking it away.
I'll have to tell her that.
On T.V. the other night
the South Bronx had no life

I could recognize.
The larvae of thieves in the gutters.
A small apocalypse.
Someday I'll have to tell my daughter
about the Bronx
before she walks through it,
though the Bronx might be everywhere
by then.
Here, the crocuses are coming up
and there are kittens by her bed.
This loveliness is hers by birth.
If I bring her up right
she'll hate that fact in a few years.
Is that true? Well, then
the people born into midnight—
they'll hate it for her.
Just love her, my wife says.
And I want to pull the covers over my head.

The Man Who Never Loses His Balance

He walks the high wire in his sleep.
The tent is blue, it is perpetual
afternoon. He is walking between
the open legs of his mother
and the grave. Always. The audience knows this
is out of their hands. The audience
is fathers whose kites are lost, children
who want to be terrified into joy.
He is so high above them, so capable
(with a single, calculated move)
of making them care for him
that he's sick of the risks
he never really takes.
The tent is blue. Outside is a world
that is blue. Inside him
a blueness that could crack
like china if he ever hit bottom.
Every performance, deep down,
he tries one real plunge
off to the side, where the net ends.
But it never ends.

The Capitalist's Love Letter

It was "bring a stranger" night
at the club of loners, and I
needed someone, temporarily.
In the dark on that street corner
when you said you weren't shy,
just had nothing to say, you became
my first guest. I knew I'd love
the company you wouldn't provide,
and you didn't disappoint me.

I'm writing this to you now because
no one has made me feel so alone since.
Come back. The club is becoming insidious;
I was asked for a match
on the same night someone was heard weeping.
I promise to be nothing to you.
If you wish to make love, I'll make love
this time. I'll make believe I'm in Chicago
at a convention of Fast Food operators.

Split: 1962

You hold the negative up
to the light, appreciating the shadows.
It is you and I posing
as you and I, what seems coming apart
at the seam at some hidden locus,
some meeting place of sensation and nerve.
Looking at ourselves this way
we are surrounded by the low clouds
of trees in full bloom, my hand in yours
is an erasure, perfect, oracular.

Now you take the scissors and cut me
out, keeping me for yourself.
Then you hand me
you. The sentimental we agree
has its place, if undeveloped.
I place you in my wallet
in the compartment I never use
so the light cannot touch you.
You do the same, as if it were possible
nothing could ruin us now—
so separate, almost unborn again.

Outline For a Religious Story

The hero of the story will admit he remained slack
and impotent when it was his turn on the beach,
the night that girl took everyone on.
He will tell how he then floated out to sea
without a thought of suicide, felt the mad eye
of the moon pass through him into the open brain
of the sea, and how he could feel his blood shift.
Much later he will return to the girl left by herself
among the empty six packs and small, extinct fires
and he will offer her the little
he has. She will be fixing her hair
or just fastening the belt to her slacks. Why
he will kiss her and start to remove her clothes
one by one, as if she were a person to whom ceremony
might be important, will never be explained.

For A., Who Knows It's Somewhere in the Vicinity of the Heart

No one has ever touched that place in her
her parents shut with the ice
hanging from their wrists.
She has never touched it either,
it exists like the memory of her birth—
on a dark beach somewhere,
in the back of her world.
A child once lived there, in that place.
She thinks it's a woman now, fully grown,
so wise it could forgive
her parents everything.
She knows she must touch it soon
with the sharp edge of her need
so that her husband may touch it
and call it by her name,
so that her children may someday touch it
and grow easily into their bodies.
It has taken years to realize her mind
has been a scientist in a room full of tears.
She has begun to believe in explosions
one can arrive at, just in time.

Scenario

Bring on the mandolins and
let the waiter serve piña coladas
with enormous straws.
Call this Cafe del Amor
and when sex intrudes
let no more than a gesture
end the tension, the guesswork.
And the woman it comes from
who vaguely had Yes
in the back of her mind, let's say
she's happy it's settled.
Let the quiet that follows
be heightened or disturbed
by such snapshots the mind takes
in advance, and let the waiter's genius be
that the check arrives, unasked.
Notice how the mandolins
presage the imminence of departure,
how the man and woman rise
as if the music had been a paradigm
for the hum in their thighs.
Let them know this moment
is theirs, and let them leave

with the kind of grace
only the awkward-in-love can have.
Bring on that sliver of a moon
and let the scud that crosses it
suggest an old, celestial boredom.
Bring on the coldness of hands,
the momentary passing
of inevitable doubt.
But let a cab be waiting
and let them make their way as best they can
toward each other and home,
toward different music or none at all
and the odds.

If Once In Silence

If once in silence you received a slap
and took it into yourself and smothered it
and said to yourself "The slap ends
with me" and smiled
and flaunted your blazing cheek,
and if the person who slapped you
left awkwardly carrying his hand
like a tail, confused by such
Christianity in the streets

and if, now, ten years later, you've learned
you were a philosophical hotdog
and he the bullyboy performing
his raw, historical role
and if you realize the slap still lives
within you like a hundred slaps,
that there's a spring in your fist

and if violence is still
the progenitor of violence
and you know this, and despise how
what you know stops your fist
when the spring releases

let's have a drink together sometime
let's talk about how it was
before experience, before the mind grew
into a bigger house, all those doors
and a fireplace

Any Time

Before dawn, before wind, when quiet is itself
a noise, how often I lie half-awake
restless, the little I-Want-Everything drum
pounding in my chest. Elsewhere
truckers already making time
on empty roads; Rocky's all-night bar
starting to fill with men
just off night jobs, winding down.
I'm full of plans, but I'm rising
and falling back, gravity
pulling me deeper into the white valleys
of my pillow, the world saying *sleep, sleep.*

Building a Person

With the leftovers and etcetera of the poor
we can build a skeleton—
chicken bones and gruel (for glue)
and perhaps the remains

of a slim cat on a skewer
for the spine.
Does anyone have a heart
for the heart we need

to give the skeleton feelings?
The hearts of the poor are always
too large or too shriveled,
but we believe a good heart

can be created. We are talking about
what appears extra
in this world— such as the tongues
of the deaf and dumb—

for muscletone and texture.
Hearts are rare these days
(at the dump
we could only find a rib cage)

and sometimes we've needed a scalpel
to locate scruples.
Still, the poor make the best kind
of orphan and orphans will often

trade crucial parts of their bodies
for a home. Already, our skeleton
is looking more human, and the rich
who pass by this vacant lot

where we are building   are interested.
They've donated the used parts
of their servants, even a brain
has come in from a downstairs maid

who (it was said) split open her head
by accident. They want a plaque made
and their names engraved and the plaque
affixed to the body. This, of course,

is not impossible. Old tin cans
from the poor's garbage could be flattened
and everyone, when it comes
to bodies, is an amateur engraver.

Soon (as planned) the Missing Person's Squad
will stop by with folks
who have lost their loved ones.
The bidding will start.

The auctioneer will say: Remember,
it takes money to maintain a person.
And, as always, the same folks
will go home emptyhanded.

Beached Whales Off Margate

One day they just started rolling up,
six pilot whales from way out.
Two hundred people pushed three of them back, oh
it took hours. I tell you all this
because two hundred people usually hurt
what they touch. But not this time.
After it was done, they all stood around
for a while, like the humans they used to be,
lamenting the three who were dead.
Separateness set in slowly; an aerial shot
would have shown a group moving away
from its center, leaving in ones and twos
toward their large, inconsiderate houses.

Belly Dancer at the Hotel Jerome

Disguised as an Arab, the bouzouki player
introduces her as Fatima, but she's blonde,
midwestern, learned to move we suspect
in Continuing Education, Tuesdays, some hip
college town.
We're ready to laugh, this is Aspen
Colorado, cocaine and blue valium
the local hard liquor, and we
with snifters of Metaxa in our hands,
part of the incongruous
that passes for harmony here.
But she's good. When she lets her hair loose,
beautiful. So we revise:
summer vacations, perhaps, in Morocco
or an Egyptian lover, or both.
This much we know:
no Protestant has moved like this
since the flames stopped licking their ankles.
Men rise from dinner tables
to stick dollar bills where their eyes
have been. One slips a five
in her cleavage. When she gets to us
she's dangling money
with a carelessness so vast
it's art, something perfected, all her bones
floating in milk.
The fake Arabs on bongos and bouzouki are real
musicians, urging her, whispering
"Fatima, Fatima," into the mike
and it's true, she has danced the mockery out
of that wrong name in this unlikely place,
she's Fatima and the cheap, conspicuous dreams
are ours, rising now, as bravos.

The Muse

Las Vegas, 1976

I was prepared
to show her the Sahara or the Dunes
or point her toward the desert.
She had angled over to me
like someone seeking directions,
but when she slid her window open
and said "Blow job, 30 dollars",
I stared at her, speechless,
and she drove off
down the Strip in her late model
Vega.

Back in the hotel room I played it
all out, witnessed from the distant
tower of my head how she would have
done it, how I might have paid her
in chips and said "Thank you",
how we both would have moved
into the next moment of our lives, unmoved,
some door clicking shut.

I had been staying even, small bets
and the kind of luck that's a visitor
who won't sit down, coat still on,
eyes that have no eyes
for yours. I counted out thirty dollars,
knowing it had already been lost
and took off with it in my fist
to the sweet casino below.
The wheel spun; I had it all
on black and it was black,
and I was playing with her money now.

The Gambler at Home

Everyone's asleep. The heat is off
for the time being. Horses run
the walls of his house, always
coming from behind. He pronounces
their names until they become pure
meaningless sound like prayer
spoken since youth. His information
is inside. His needs are secrets
he can only share with crowds.
And now he feels it again
somewhere in his stomach—
that absence growing palpable.
Ragged zeroes when he smokes.

How can his family know
when he says *the unlit room*
he means the moment before loss.
Or when he puts his arms around them
he's thinking *one less empty space.*
It's late and cold and part of him
knows the world is gorgeous
in its disregard, but cruel enough
to kiss you now and then.
That part of him would take the kiss
and run. Never bet again.
That's a promise, he says, halfway
to forgetfulness and the dream
where the favorite fades
and despair's wild hunch comes on.

Directions

The yogis return from the ashram
   in their loose whites, in their
      pink-cheeked radiances.

Here in the world of distraction
   where I live, I've been
      downing scotch and eating

the flesh of an animal. That's
   how it is. I love them
      and they love me—

one of them is the woman I married
   long ago when she was as provocative
      as corruption, the other

an old jock friend
   shedding his skin.
      They tell me the dross

they've cast off, just this weekend,
   what Guruji said about ego
      (that trickster in us

with a brilliant shield), how the
   breaths they've learned
      take them into the hidden

chakras of the heart.
   Oh, I'm the wild renunciate
      of nothing, happy they're happy,

but feeling more like a wastrel every minute.
   I pour myself a drink, try to get
      the talk around to the NCAA

playoffs, a shot at the buzzer
   that made me leap out of my seat.
      It's useless, they're so loving today

they love everything I say
   indiscriminately, they think in time
      maya will lift its veil,

that I'll finally make a plan
   that has a path. As I put my arms
      around them, I'm thinking

Christs, the sinners have no choice
   but to hang you up there
      everytime you make them feel how fat

they are, those bones of yours sticking out
   like wisdom we can neither afford
      nor bear, and I start to dance

around the room in circles, leading them,
   and now they are dancing,
      leading me, and we're each going

where our bodies take us, into what
   recesses, what
      next steps.

Greenwich Village: A Memory

I got pockets.
I got no money

      —My 2½ year old

Men with bottles in paperbags
would languish in my doorway

and everywhere the gay shirts of the poor
blossomed around the armpits.

Two guys who sized me up said
How about a buck for the brothers Karamazov?

A lady with 54 pennies shaking in her hand
said *2 cents more would do it.*

I had pockets, and the sounds in them
were little bells as I walked

past the vague faces that looked
like aerial shots of Utah taken at twilight.

They all had pockets, but that's all.
Late at night you could see their hands

in them, fingering the stale air
and you knew they were dreaming

of jackpots and windfalls and the
sweet oblivion after the eyes roll.

Once I almost offered my bed
to a man out cold against a hydrant, but this

was a block of many homeless, hungry men.
What would become of me?

I was a bookish man and the books were full
of saints who went mad or died young.

Sister

The sister I never had
enters my wife when I am
sleeping next to her
So many times
I've watched my sister
come from her separate room
the room that long ago
in a house of brothers
was an extra room
down the hall from where
I would dream her alive
She climbs into bed
on my wife's side
and I touch my wife awake
for now my sister and she
are the woman I must talk to
about incompleteness and love
Awake she doesn't know
my sister is in her
she doesn't know why my embrace
has so much gratefulness in it
why my questions are all
whispered as if
a father could overhear us
She thinks I want to
make love but I remove
her hand and hold it
ask another question
about high school and loss
the kind of loss

that repeats itself every day
like being born
without a leg
I watch my sister leave
as my wife takes me
in her arms says hush
you've been talking again
sleep now
and I curl into her
as if it were possible
she could be everything to me
alone like this
just ourselves

Tortures

My father used to tell me bamboo
grows so fast
the Japanese would sharpen its edges
and spread-eagle a prisoner

above it. It was a lousy torture,
he'd confess anything, secret bombs,
secret dreams, secret movements planned
for secret warships, as the point of it

came within inches. There were no heroes,
only prisoners who loved their country
more than their genitals,
and my father felt hero was the wrong word

for *them*. Finally, so many things
were confessed, Japanese Intelligence ordered
an end to it, said the single admission
was always truer

than a list of truths, and so
a water torture was instigated
which produced insanity, a babbling
about one's childhood and in amongst it

something like "Amphibian landing at
0800 on the 12th". Never failed.
On the other hand, my father said,
we would put prisoners in lockers

and hit the lockers with baseball bats
and other measures lacking in subtlety
or absolute terror. We could have lost
the war, he said.

A Concise History of the Future

The sky was finished
one day it just turned white
and the next all we had over us
were our hats and the stars
burned for hours where they fell
and the moon was shot
in a card game and never seen again
Something else
would take its place, we thought,
but nothing did it was bad
for the birds it was bad for heaven
priests began to look into
the odd weather of their hearts
began to say maybe and perhaps
the sky was just low air now
colorless as an unspoken word
Everyone would have to make
his own sky, the existentialists said,
the pessimists cried
we must prepare for the end
When the sun was found in a heap
its wires gone and adults
taking flying leaps into it
something had to be done
We prayed to our shadows for clouds
we saved our breath
we hired a poet to invent

a sky as convincing as our souls
which we believed in
but had never seen
He invented a sky of dreams instead
different every day
a kaleidoscope of lost desires
a panoply of whim and doubt
Everyone gave up his job
to dream the sky we've been doing this
for years now
coveting little pieces of light.

Notes Toward a 20th Century Newsreel

In Madagascar someone is dreaming
   of Hackensack, and knives with pearl handles
     made in the Casbah

are getting into
   the open sewers of Newark and this is
     "how things are".

Turn over a dead Mexican
   and find his unidentical twin
     in Bangkok.

Turn over today and there is
   history with its flag
     of bandages.

Oh the places with soft sounds
   are murderous and the places
     with hard sounds

are murderous; the difference is
   the pavement is warmer, say,
     in Guatamala than it is in Minsk

and in putting together the fragments
   the job is not to overlook
     even that.

Notice who kisses who in Sicily
   and years later find his brother
     face down in the movies.

Learn to anticipate. Be there,
   which is anyplace,
     when it happens.

Here and There

Here and there nightfall
without fanfare
presses down, utterly
expected, not an omen in sight.
Here and there a husband
at the usual time
goes to bed with his wife
and doesn't dream of other women.
Occasionally a terrible sigh
is heard, the kind that is
theatrical, to be ignored.
Or a car backfires
and reminds us of a car
backfiring, not of a gunshot.
Here and there a man says
what he means and people hear him
and are not confused.
Here and there a missing teenage girl
comes home unscarred.
Sometimes dawn just brings another
day, full of minor
pleasures and small complaints.
And when the newspaper arrives
with the world,
people make kindling of it
and sit together while it burns.

A Circus of Needs

In his circus of needs—
   desire and the limitations
    of desire,

those empty spaces
   beyond his fingertips
    and the travel into them,

the ephemera of such arrivals,
   the next place to go.
    There was no tent, no arena,

just these private little efforts
   to fulfill himself, not unlike
    yours, or anyone's.

He wanted to be women
   now and then, half knowing
    the woman in him

was the exile whose messages
   couldn't be stopped.
    He wanted to be a you,

some second person
   without a name or an address
    and, like you (because he wanted

everything), he wanted to be in love
   but love would never stay
      where it had begun.

He didn't want to be
   this thin man whose desires
      were barely covered by skin,

standing absolutely still.
   But everytime he moved
      there was another place to go,

and everytime sadness would arrive
   with its wonderful cocoon—
      not even that would last.

II

I am the normal man, gone public

—from *Confessions of a Peeping Tom*

Weatherman

Tonight I've decided to tell you, friends,
how much bad weather excites me.
I love the way it moves
state to state, and though I seem to rejoice
when it blows out to sea, that's just showbiz,
I'd like it to perch off the Carolinas
or double back across the nation,
and I know some of you feel the same.
Something in me responds to a low
and I'm sorry, I can watch the footage
from tornado damage all evening.
I know you too like to see cars off the road,
families disconnected, I know when you sigh
and say "How sad" your heart is thumping
to a tune you hardly understand. Friends,
this is a communication tonight,
not a broadcast. Here in the East
where no weather originates, where everything
moves toward us and so little arrives;
here, where we're forced to watch things
break up, or swerve toward Erie, what is it
that has turned in us, that has turned in me?
All I know is I can't deny the secret
happiness when a system moves across Nebraska
as I thought I would, paralyzing North Platte,
the National Guard called out, wind chill
(just the words *wind chill*) plunging
into my imagination. And you who live out there
where weather is a fact of life, don't you
secretly love it and look forward to it,
don't you love to survive it? And I mean *love*.
When I lived in Minnesota half my life
was the weather. A blizzard was me
and the blizzard. A tornado meant
the southwest corner of my basement

huddled with loved ones. Never have I been
so happy. It is we in the East I worry about;
only in August when the hurricanes wend up
from the Bahamas are our bodies truly connected
to our minds. Only then can devastation
make our lives less academic, only then
can we trace a path that leads directly
to ourselves.
    So tonight I wanted to confess to you,
voyeurs and participants alike,
I wanted to let you know I know
the deep thrill of a five day forecast,
of a science so inexact
we learn to trust accident after accident.
Believe me, the scattered highs across
the country will not arrive
any time close to schedule. And they will not
give you any lasting pleasure. Frankly,
I'll be bored if a system, say, out of Manitoba
doesn't push in and complicate everything.
Right now there's a disturbance around the Panhandle
that could be a big one. In the days ahead
I'll follow it for you, I'll watch it the way
a Christian Scientist watches virulence in a leg wound,
and if things turn bad or something perverse
gets into me, I'm sure you'll understand
that's how things are and I am,
that's the weather, some of the time.

Imagine: A Stolen Kiss

transported over the State Line,
and a woman waking somewhere
discovering a kiss of hers

is missing, look at her
check her entire body
to see if any love was lost

and the man now, safe,
holding up the kiss, examining it,
putting it with the others.

Anatomy Lesson: A School For Boys

Here we have the ordinary wrist
between arm and hand, a connection as old
but less interesting than the clavicle
linking scapula and sternum. And here,
the joint called knee, in the middle
of the leg— femur, tibia, patella—
my students, is no Latin
double play combination. You must learn
to be precise. Just as a quadroon
is not fully a black man, and a fingerprint
reveals but is *not* a fingertip, no anklebone
ever slew a giant or should be confused
with an ass. I mention this because
some of you on the last exam wrote
you could not tell the fibula from the truth
and though this may have been a joke
it was a bad joke, evasive, crass,
like mistaking the pudenda with a place
from which one speaks. No more of it, please.
Here we have the anus and its sphincter—
common sources of laughter, I know—
but sophisticated, capable of magic.
And here, the penis which you must learn
is no weapon, the part of your body
whose natural link is outside of it, but the vagina
is another class entirely, a whole afternoon,
a lifetime. Let's move to the thorax, that cavity
in which the heart and lungs lie.
It, too, is very beautiful,
a place unto itself, where nighttime
is perpetual and surgery common.
Everything is connected or wishes to be
connected. I can't stress that enough.
For tomorrow, read about the magnificence
of the elbow. For Thursday, the nape and the spine.

Let's See If I Have it Right

I kiss these before I kiss that,
then I wait to see
if you're the kind who'll kiss this.
If you're not I go on kissing
these and that, careful always
to place my hands where my lips
are not. However, if you do kiss this
I can choose to lie back
and watch or arrange myself
in such a way so I can kiss that
while you're kissing this so that
kissing is no longer the exact word.
Around this time, as I recall,
every part of speech is ready
for every other part, whether it speaks
or not, and that and sometimes
the other thing is entered by this
with its single accurate eye
and *still* there are various options
and contingencies which (it is said)
I will remember before the time comes
for this to come or that kingdom
of yours to come, and I think
I'm allowed to touch these
if I can reach them, which always
is supposed to depend.

Essay on Sanity

I am tired of hearing the insane
   lauded for their clear
      thinking. If they do

get to the reddest heart of things
   it's because they can't see
      the world of appearances,

where you are, struggling to separate
   the difficult jewel from the
      chalcedony that surrounds it.

And I love the world
   of appearances with its blue veils
      its bright tintinnabulations, I

wouldn't give it up for that dark laser
   the mad point
      in no special direction.

(Except, of course,
   for an afternoon of white light
      with you somewhere.)

The point is you, who romanticize
   those who are wise and sad
      and tortured, *you* wouldn't

want to be *them*. And, sure,
   we are sad too in our daily indifference
      to the moon inside us, in

our sleeping bodies, but there is
   a difference— it is, say,
      having breakfast with someone

    you love, the calm small ordinary
        exchanges between people
           who know knives

every once in a while are *not*
    the silvercoated castrati
        of their worst dreams. People who

can read a book or newspaper, play
    ball or attend an orgy, who can do
        all these without carrying around

a picture of that cracked ceiling and its
    one enormous spider, who can do
        everything without the fear

that their heads can be entered
    by a dark god, a terrible
        flickering clarity.

Let us not romanticize them! They
    who can't return to the small talk
        of any given evening.

            ****

Who is sane is a question
    of resistance, the mind saying No
        to the sanctioned lies, the body

speaking up to the inner ear
    that has been educated to hear it.
        It is a question

of moments; people in the first rush
   of love are the most sane,
      the most able to feel their way

into importance. When the sign says
   Underarm Deodorants, they will put
      their tongues into each other's

armpits. When someone publishes a treatise
   on love, theirs will be the pantomime
      that mocks it— just as

the truly sane person will mock
   this poem by simply walking
      into any room!

Nevertheless it is with our poems
   that we must visit ourselves, who are
      neither here

nor there. And those never astonished
   by their own humanity, smack
      in the arid middle.

But I am tired of insanity
   being attributed to the middle
      class. Even *they* know the real issue

is lack of courage, a standing still
   while the distant children
      of their desires cry out

from a burning building. Insight
   is the awful burden. They know this.
      To be sane, perhaps, is to bring it

to the magnificent thin-as-ice world
   of appearances, making sure the rope
      that keeps you from the abyss

is secured around your waist,
   so you're free enough
      to know everything superficial

is as real as that which
   it conceals. The mad, those who
      are so beautiful

when years later we read what they said,
   reject the smile for the teeth
      behind it, cannot help

themselves, remind us always,
   like conscience, they are
      terrible companions.

Argument

"There's no such thing as human nature."
   —a Marxist, in conversation

Hubris was the word I wanted
and if I had found it
I could have strategically confessed
to my own: how, when I lived in New York

I believed I knew everything
but now know so much more.
But I said perversity was the first human
constant, and he frowned, this man I loved

for his nature, human and fine
and flawed. I wanted to say it's human nature
to create a politics so humane
it excludes half the world,

I wanted to say friendship, unlike history,
is what happens when two forces meet
and grow gentle— that's our history—
but I insisted on the perverse

and that wouldn't do,
he wasn't as perverse as I,
I should have named four or five
of the Seven Deadly Sins and said

when lust is culturally abolished
I'll be its guerilla priest
gathering followers in the hills.
I should have said, friend,

though it's human nature to forgive
as well as to never forgive,
we'll survive this argument,
it's human nature

to say No
to any self-assured Yes,
to make peace, to lie down happily
in strange beds.

III

In a Dream of Horses

I think I loved the palomino best,
though the roan had the shoulders
of a horse that went wire to wire
for me once. This time
just some sleepy motion
around the moon, while the stars watched.
The night gave way
to the horses and kept on
closing up behind them. After a while
I was on the palomino. It was a race
for who could go slowest and yet
not break stride. Within the dream
I remember dreaming the postponement
of dawn, and promptly woke
as if I had broken some rule.
You were awake beside me
and in the retelling I put you
on the roan and added a forest,
feeling you wouldn't believe
I'd be riding alone in a dream,
in a dream of such obvious charm,
if I could help it.

Backyard

The birds fold back
>   their wings, give permission
>   to the dark.

And we, who have forgotten
>   the old rituals at sunset,
>   are simply overtaken.

Martinis, blindness.
>   No words to make the night
>   our own.

Modern Fable

For years the stars were not
visible to the city
so parents
read myths of stars
to their children at bedtime
They no longer believed
what they read
though it pleased
their sense of nostalgia
and it pleased their children
who brought the stars
into themselves like a thousand
shining hearts
When the children grew up
and moved to the country
there were the stars!
and it was as if
a story had come true
but it wasn't their story
and they called home
with the world in their throats
the bittersweet news

Introduction to the 20th Century

The conveyor belts bearing hubcaps and loneliness
were everywhere, and the invisible ruts in the air
could transport you for a lifetime
if you weren't careful. Monotony had a hair trigger
and there were machines that sounded like the sea
and put you to sleep if the jackhammers were thumping.
Oh, when the sun broke through the pink haze
of our luxuries, lovers were seen falling into the same
ancient swoon. And the ledgers of motels
grew spectacular with aliases, there was no way
to escape the day-glo and boldface, the suburbs
crowded with manuals.

Yet some of us were happy for hours, days, weeks.
Even in the subways there were people to love,
there were children who ripped apart their mothers
to get into the world, and the mothers called them
Daughter or Son, and the fathers got drunk
and felt they had a say in the universe.
This would happen every day! And for every death
there was a building or a poem. For every
lame god a rhythm and a hunch, something local
we could possibly trust. We learned to put
history books down gently on the table.
If curious, we asked a Jew about Hitler
or invented our own satisfactory monster.
In difficult times, we came to understand,
it's the personal and only the personal that matters.

Creating the Conditions

I enter the building which is no more
than these blueprints in my hand
which shape themselves around me.
If you appear, it is you

I'm looking for.
Let there be disembodied catcalls
for suspense. Let each door
be marked Exit and Entrance.

Here's a marble pillar
where you could conceal yourself.
Here, an escalator that runs
into my arms.

I have created everything
but you, and your next move.
If you appear, so be it.
If nothing, I will lie down

with nothing and form the kiss
that will not be received.
Such are the rules; I didn't make them:
when love fails

absurdity begins, takes up
where it left off before love began
once upon a time
when conditions were just right,

like now.
Already, I can feel my desire grow
a conservative edge, my body wish
to step backward.

Surely if you were to appear
out of the menace and ennui
you would be so brave,
so dark,

who could ever properly love you?
Who could not try to?
Never before have I
planned it so carefully,

left so much room for you
to take on flesh, or deny your own
existence. This is the fear
I've dreamt of, elements of awe

in it, a meeting in a place
that hardly exists, something nameless
and perhaps looking for a name
breathing in the hushed, thin air.

The Magician's Dream

I pull this from nowhere, from
   out of the hips of roses,
     from the scar

in the sky. It is this,
   what I'm holding, what you can't see,
     this lovely piece

of thisness, this body of wild claim
   I'd like you to care about.
     Imagine this, for example.

Or imagine this: earthlight bottled
   in a factory near Newark and sold
     to the stars. What I have here

is the commodity of our time, *none*
   of the above, that which always follows
     simple A,B,C, like cruelty.

It is none of your business either.
   That's why there's a possibility
     you'll care about it, this shadow

wearing a cloak in a grey world, this
   self-cancelling mandrake root
     that will not produce

a single birth. I hold it up to you now
   so that you won't see it.
     Look, it's gone

and all this time you haven't left
   your seats. Confess. All you ever cared about
     was me.

Danse Manhattanique

Let us know each other by this
dance, barefoot, over bits of glass.
Let our arms
discover what's in the air
around us, how much resistance,
what passages, our fingertips alive
to high frequencies, doubts, jazz.
Let's move
to the jugular pulse of our lives,
shake our asses
to the sound of petty crime,
a cash register opening,
a libido humming
in a nearby room.
And when we return to our chairs,
the dance floor
arid with our absence,
let's invent the brawl
that starts at the bar— two men, say,
who need the exercise,
let's conjure the bloodbeat,
the contagion of violence,
and slip out into the street
with such things behind us,
having done and survived them.
Let's then (for a moment,
in our minds) take the Thruway upstate
and arrive at a place
where good days slide so easily
into the bad they deprive us
of grand gestures.
Let there be trees. Vacancies
for belief. The sky, perhaps,
as it once was.

The Manhattanite's Dream

The maniac's heart wasn't in it.
So they hired a zealot.
He shook the quiet
out of the calm.
Then entered it.
And there were followers.

The woman who had been
with a thousand men became angelic.
So they hired a woman
who had been with none.
Softness under her
meant lack of courage.
Anything that didn't come
she'd pull.

They hired a mass murderer
who did it barehanded.
The sadist with his single whip
was discarded.
They advertised for someone
with far-reaching obsessions.
Two one-armed men
arrived with her suitcase.

And then they were ready.

They came to your apartment.
They replaced your wife
with a photograph from Dachau.
They converted your kids.
Then everyone played Daddy
from ankle to skull.

And the neighbors who hear everything
were in Bermuda.
And all the police were in the Rockaways
for a policeman's funeral.

Let's Say

Let's say the dark, one night,
is no metaphor for the dark
and men in sharkskin suits are
real men and all their women
real women dressed to kill.
Let's say your small car is
parked in the unmetaphorical dark
and you're aware of characters
who suddenly distinguish themselves
from lampposts but let's say
you can confront your fear
as a sleepwalker confronts stairs—
with an ignorance
graced by years of practice.
Let's say, then, you make it to your car
choosing to believe

the switchblade which might have opened
a second ago
was the man in the sharkskin suit
clicking his tongue
against the roof of his mouth.
And the hand that reached from the back seat
to cover your mouth
was nothing but a flash
from a movie you saw last week.
Let's say you believe you're safe now
because none of your blood is
making roses on the floor
and your headlights have come on
in this real dark

and you see where you're going.
And let's say the obligatory problem
with the starter
doesn't occur, the typical whisper
from an unclaimed part of yourself
is found to be air
slipping in from the vent.
Let's even say
you're moving along nicely now
on the boulevard where harm itself
is a local attraction,
making all the staggered lights, whistling
as if escape
or the illusion of escape
were a kind of normalcy,
almost a life, here in the city.

This Late In the Century

I walk the streets
always a gesture away from contact,
ungiven gifts, first words
it would seem foolish to say.

And then I forget about it all
and go about my half-desired loneliness,
back to the body's asylum
way back here where the movie

of the world is playing and all of us
are watching one seat apart.
Sometimes even after I return home
the stranger I am

will find those pockets
of collapsed air
where not even kisses
can find him. Other times

I watch any two of us
form the modern we
out of our separate lives;
I bring my distances, say,

to yours, you bring yours to mine,
and with such safety
the first words, the lovely intimate
incomplete sentence.

A Few Nights and Days

He foresaw a lagoon
cut off from its larger body,
capillaries floating like plankton
in a cadaver, a man with his arms
joyously around men and women...

When he woke it was a Tuesday,
the porchlight still on
and umbrage in the air
over breakfast; the woman he loved
had her eyes closed
looking for holes in his arguments.
He muffled his mouth, hating her,
wondering if she knew she'd be dead
in thirty or forty years,
hating himself and the stone wall
he could build in seconds
around his heart, hating the nationtalk,
the journalism between people
who simply want to touch.

His daughter came in with the
alphabet in her mouth;
how, out of love, he squeezed her
until she was breathless—
how, if she were Vietnamese
and on the run, beyond hunger,
scabbed, whimpering,
he might, out of love, squeeze her
until she was dead.
And then it was Wednesday and Thursday

and every morning the porchlight
a dull beacon in the sun.

* * *

He dreamed the last suck
of a falling star, that intake
of air before one begins
to dazzle the world—
and the regular breath
of people everywhere
contemplating insurance. . .

And he found himself
on the edge of nothing
in particular, in the middle
of a bed big enough for three victims
of the six-o'clock news.
He made love to his wife
whispering *this is how you steal
moments from the end of your life*
and they knocked the clock off the nighttable
the covers onto the floor
and the orphans
took their big eyes elsewhere.

But only for a while.
There were satellites near the moon
reporting everything,
children wanting to know
why squirrels didn't look both ways
before cars hit them,

the ordinary desolation
of handshakes and lunches.
Not even sex or his natural capacity
for self-deception did much good
anymore.

On the last day of the week
in a year in a lifetime of last days
he left his house
daydreaming his shadow
had shed its dark clothes.
The streets were crowded.
He saw the flesh of beautiful women—
all flesh— as flesh that is dying,
but he said to himself *every touch
is a renewal, every touch is
a renewal*

and he touched no one.

Fable of the Unsharable Secrets of the Universe

He couldn't sleep,
the windows were rattling
and when he got up to secure them
he saw, by accident, all the stars a man
with a naked eye is allowed to see,
scattered like dice,
and heard an owl interrogate the night.
                        His wife,
awakened by the absence of noise,
heard the door shut
and saw her husband disappear
down the path they had never
given a name. He should have left
the rattle, she thought, or a word.
The silence was a collision seen
far, far off.
                      He came back
for breakfast, harmless scratches on his face,
and what looked like moondust on his hands
could as easily have been chilblains
from the cold. When his wife said "Well...?",
he said "Let's not get philosophical,
pass the honey, I need something sweet
in my mouth."

...le of the Water Merchants

...rchants came
...ter pass
...
...ddicted
...eatened
...nd the people
...ns and placed them
...eir feet.
... merchants had carved
...ds out of wood
... to the river bank.
The people said
...stes different now"
...r merchants replied "What you
..., friends, is progress",
...people began to love it
...e the merchants everything they wanted.

Fable of the Mad and the Respectable

One day on a crowded street, for no reason,
his laughter blooms out of control,
and people shake their heads
with the cold lament of superiors
and walk away.
And his laughter grows silent
as violets and just as dark
and he wants to climb with it
to a window far above it all.
He enters a building
and the people walking away
turn and watch him, shaking their heads.
They whisper *unanimous, unanimous,*
and begin to write things on index cards.
And his laughter closes
on itself, his lips tight and pink.
And the people walking away
are still walking away, past the poor
to whom they say: *Poor.* Past small birds
which they name: *Small Birds,*
shaking their heads all the time.
And now, at that window far above it all,
he feels his laughter break like menses
and something louder than confetti
comes down.

The Man Who Loves Hegel

It's been no fun for him, ever since
the pulpit's throttle
got publicly stuck.
No joy disobeying the powerless.
Once, he struggled his flesh
beyond guilt, flipped through
the prayerwheel of desire,
joined the angels down the block
who had gang wars.
Didn't believe in anything
he couldn't touch.

Now that everybody's doing
the secular dance,
the easily mastered steps,
he dreams of entering
the ancient cockpit, hands full
of modern grease, for the fun of it.
He dreams of lifting up
whatever can get off the ground,
of doing for the invisible
what Marianne Moore did for bats
hanging upside down.

Already, though, he feels the old pull
back, the attraction
of the opposite as it strolls naked
into the church, saying
come with me for a while.

Dream

He becomes very small like a genie
and returns to that paradise of sloth,
his mother's womb. All he would like
is crawl space and to force blood again
with that head of his.
                    He knows the mother's body
is always prepared for such returns.
An umbilical cord hangs precisely
where it should. Her breasts are ready
to swell with warm milk
for his occasional journeys
                back and forth.
He is pain and he knows it
and this is the red love everybody wants.
And the secrets and tears his mother has
held in, how they drip down like evidence
against his father.

Modern Dance Class

The difficulties of grace.
How first the body must learn
the elementary extensions,
the possibilities it knew
as a child, unnatural now—
wacky as obedience lessons
for a cat.
The instructor looks at me
the way gas station attendants
look at tires whose treads are gone;
I imagine he's thinking "Oh
get a new one, a man could die
with a body like that".
I know grace
is what occurs after technique
has been loved a long while
and then forgotten.
So I take the steps,
I reach as far as I can reach.
My thighs are muscled
from sports in which opponents
were other than myself,
my arms have no history
of holding themselves in air
without bringing something back.
But I remember a fat girl
whose grace was the loveliness
with which she carried her burden.
I knew a stutterer whose poems
were sailboats and wind.
But I'm neither good
nor driven, I just want to be

magnificent as if by magic
the way a teenager does.
By now, the instructor has
turned his head, I'm his toad
among butterflies,
he can't bear to look.
I'm so wrong for this
in my leotard
I'm thinking my cock
is a nipple under a wet blouse,
everybody's staring at it,
my balls are Christmas
for the loneliest person in class.
Soon he calls it a day,
says "practice or stuff it"
and walks off.
I dress slowly, thinking how much better
I might have said that.

The Obsession

I decided to call the dark
by its right color
so when it came down on us
or when it was in the house
I could say navy blue
is upon us or obsidian has come
with its black ice,
I could know the quality
of what touched us.

It started as an experiment,
almost a joke,
but soon I was wondering about dusk,
trying to remember how often
I'd driven home in it,
driven by it, shadow's breath,
a weight that wasn't
quite there.
I dimmed the lights in the livingroom,
it couldn't be simulated;
I walked out into it,
a simultaneous goodbye
on a street corner.

The dark was less elusive.
After all, the synonym for brain

is grey-matter, and who isn't
the brain's amateur, dusk's
confused traveler?
I tried to adjust my eyes.
It was midnight, the midnight
that has tried to myth us
into love or crime, deceive us
into not seeing it.
I wanted to decide what part of the dark
is chilling, the correct color
for desolate.
You were with me.
I was holding your hand;
at another time of my life
we could have walked into the sunset.

The Worrier

So he wouldn't think of his children
he kept ordinary things around him,
things that wouldn't fail
or if they would, would not
be weeped over: buck-ninety-five
dime novels, a black and white
television, nothing
so lamentable as children.
Even the most extraordinary of children,
which his were not, would fail
some false dream you had for them.
They would grow pubic hair and desires
no father could ignore
or do anything about—
no, he wanted nothing nearby
as lamentable as children or lap dogs
or even big dogs who curl
near your feet who die like parents
just when you've learned to live with them.
He liked things that were guaranteed—
the stereo's diamond needle, stone-ware
plates, he would have liked classics
if he had known their definition.
These were not ordinary
but ordinary comforts, dull after a while

like the perfectly insured body
of an athlete.
And that was how he wanted it
in his landscape of wishes.
All his children had been kidnapped
and hit by cars, oh so many times,
and still they came down each morning
from their bedrooms, incarnations of themselves,
bearing their lovely, intolerable futures
and the dog whined for food
and it was ghostly to live like this, he felt,
if only the dog were a tea-kettle
singing that it was ready,
if only his children
were somebody else's, borrowed,
whose funerals he might go to
out of some vague sense of duty.

The Solitary Man's Story

That dead end street; it was
like slipping my hand into a pocket
where the dark was warm and everything
deliciously limited.
I'd go to the end, the pleasure
in the turnabout which could take hours
if I wanted it to.
And she was always there, abracadabra,
born by a wish and a rub, perfect
for as long as I could make her last.
(You would have said I was dancing
with myself, I bet.)

When they came crazed with words
like "access"
and opened the street onto those boulevards
where the fast food joints
suck in cars,

it was a kind of plunder
or at least she's gone
and I've gone looking for other dead ends
and found them
magicless and cold.

I dreamed the other night
I was a woman, my vagina a hill
I had always wanted to be king of,

balloons inside me
waiting for air.
Soon it was as if I was receiving myself,
filling and being filled,
and then I woke.

In the old neighborhood now
there's a place I can't return to.
There's a time of my life
that's gone. I know you would say
that *is* life, but fuck you.
The women I've met are so much
old news. They don't tremble
when I do. And, later,
nothing I say to them makes them
reappear.

To You, Whomever

All those grand laments
I've spoken about, ah
forget them. They were true
but no truer than yours
which I've walked away from
so many times.
Who can listen to them
unless they occur, say,
on the Avenida de la Luz
under a tumorous sky,
misfortune simply the aura
amid which you and I
smile, and go on.
So goodbye to unhappiness
which is not unusual enough
to mention. Goodbye to the lover
who pivots at the meeting place
and is never seen again.
The doctors these days
can take a little skin
from your thigh to patch up
your chest, you yourself can dial
an old number,
in a few weeks memory
will have placed her historically
between this one and that.
But instead of laments, what?
Joys? But then we would speak

so seldom. Achievements?
They translate so yawningly
into words. Please,
not the world again
with its facts and flowers,
what's there to say about it
until grief or joy makes it lean
in our direction? You must understand
goodbye is a promise
I try over and over to keep.
I had good intentions,
just remember that.
Even now, as I move toward pleasure,
I anticipate a visit so short
I've already thought of its elegy,
and how it should be sung.

Contact
For Ron Banner

Once, to make friends with friends
two blocks over was downright international.
Now I map the places
they've gone, or I've left:
Utah, Cadiz, Minnesota, Saint Bonnet.
Diminution is the way of things, sure.
I know letters turn to postcards, a note
at Christmas, a goodbye. But I say No
to the way of things. I'm crazy
to touch them so as not to lose touch.
My phone bills are the literature
of rendezvous: date, time, place—
wavelengths, connections.
My vacations are visits.
I dream of paying the air fare
of every friend since childhood
to someplace central like Chicago.
Renting the Hilton. Dress: casual.
A crazy-quilt of personalities to match
all of mine, and me the only thing
they have in common.
It's a death dream of course, a gathering
that would put my life together, an illusion
of my importance. But why not?
I've nothing but what I love
and have loved. The rest is attractive
tinsel or worse: a stoniness
when I had hoped for flesh.
Friend, whom I have lost to California,
this is dedicated to you,
who has broken off all contact.
This is to say I understand why
and cannot abide it.
So here's another first step, this poem
I will try to publish in the West
where anything used to be possible
and now, I think, is just barely.

Instead of You

I place a dead butterfly on the page,
this is called starting
with an image from real life.
It is gold and black
and, as if in some embalmer's dream,
a dusting of talc on its wings.
I have plans
for these wings. I will not let them
slip through my hands.
And if anyone is worried about how
the butterfly died, I'll tell them
my cat swatted it out of the air,
I just picked it up
and brought it to this page
with a notion of breathing
a different life into it. And I confess:
the cat's gesture was more innocent than mine.

The wings suggest nothing I want,
they are so lovely
I simply like the way they distract,
how my eye turns away from the living-
room, and the mind spins
into the silliness of Spring.
I don't want much.
Just for certain private places
to remain open to me, that's all.
But this is no time to get ephereal.
Already, in a far corner of the page,
something dark is tempting me
to pull it into the poem. One tug
and it's a bat
trapped in sunlight, rabid with fear.

There's no way to keep the ugliness out,
ever. Drops of blood

beautiful, say, on the snow.
always lead to a wound.
Can this still turn out to be a love poem?
Can I still pull you from the wreckage
and kiss your bruises, so black and gold?
Is it too late to introduce you
who was always here, the watermark,
the poem's secret?
From the start all I wanted to explain
was how things go wrong,
how the heart's an empty place
until it is filled,
and how the darkness is forever waiting
for its chance.
If I have failed, know that I was trying
to get to you in my own way,
know that my cat never swatted a butterfly,
it was I who invented and killed it,
something to talk about
instead of you.

Carnegie-Mellon Poetry

The Living and the Dead, Ann Hayes (1975)

In the Face of Descent, T. Alan Broughton (1975)

The Week the Dirigible Came, Jay Meek (1976)

Full of Lust and Good Usage, Stephen Dunn (1976)

*How I Escaped from the Labyrinth
          and Other Poems,* Philip Dacey (1977)

The Lady from the Dark Green Hills, Jim Hall (1977)

For Luck: Poems 1962-1977, H.L. Van Brunt (1977)

By the Wreckmaster's Cottage, Paula Rankin (1977)

New & Selected Poems, James Bertolino (1978)

The Sun Fetcher, Michael Dennis Browne (1978)

A Circus of Needs, Stephen Dunn (1978)

The Crowd Inside, Elizabeth Libbey (1978)

Paying Back the Sea, Philip Dow (1979)